COMPLEXITY

New works by

MARILYN HENRION

April 3 - 28, 2012

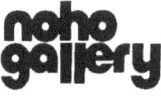

noho gallery

530 West 25 Street
New York, NY 10001
www.nohogallery.com

Photography by D. James Dee
Cover Image: Red Rock triptych

Complexity

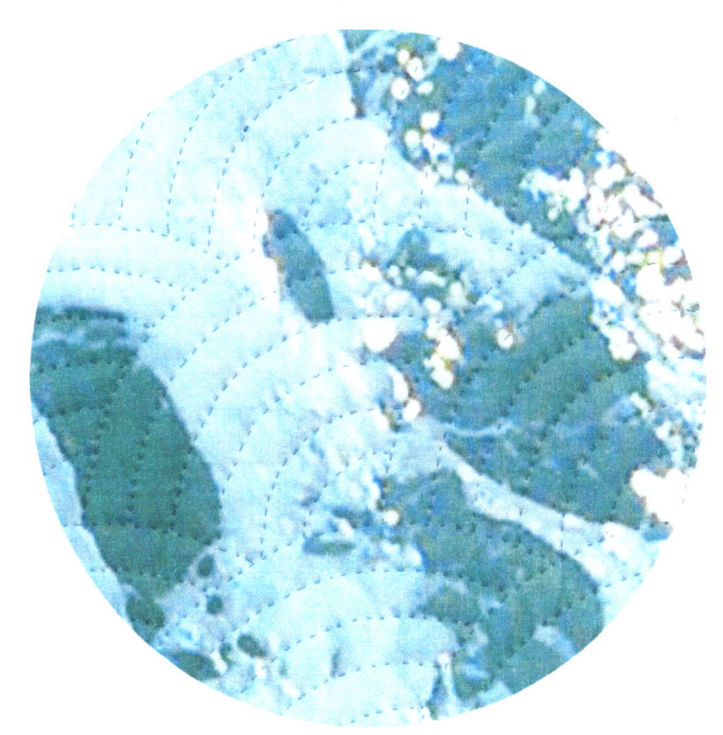

MARILYN HENRION

"Home is where one starts from. As we grow older

The world becomes stranger, the pattern more complicated

Of dead and living. Not the intense moment

Isolated, with no before and after,

But a lifetime burning in every moment

And not the lifetime of one man only

But of old stones that cannot be deciphered."

T.S. Eliot, Four Quartets

"As we begin to understand complex systems, we begin to understand that we're part of an ever-changing, interlocking, non-linear, kaleidoscopic world.......The elements always stay the same, yet they're always re-arranging themselves. So its like a kaleidoscope: the world is a matter of patterns that change, that partly repeat, but never quite repeat, that are always new and different."

William Bryan Arthur, Director of the Santa Fe Institute

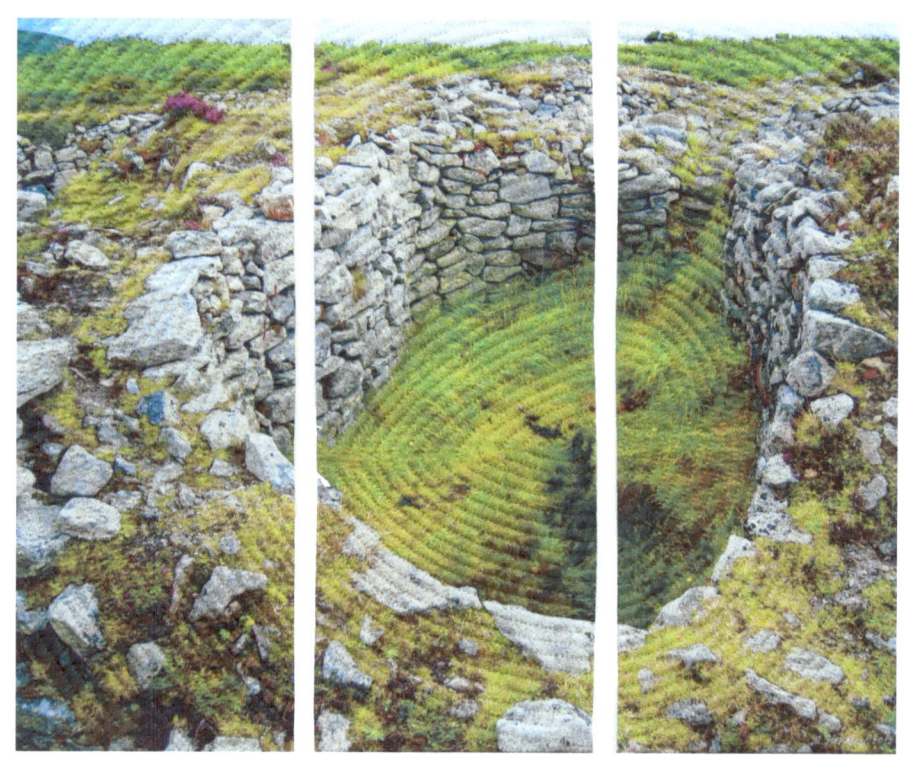

"Complexity" Takes Varied Forms In Marilyn Henrion's Triumphant New Solo Show
An essay by Ed McCormack

More than most visual artists, Marilyn Henrion has always taken inspiration from poetry. Back in the Beat era, Henrion and her husband Ed held regular literary salons in their home in Greenwich Village, at which Allen Ginsberg, Ray Bremser, and other Beat poets read. She introduces her most recent series of mixed media works, "Complexity," with a quote from T.S. Eliot's Four Quartets: "Home is where we start from. / As we grow older / The world becomes stranger, the patterns more complicated / Of dead and living. / Not the intense moment / Isolated, with no before and after, / But a lifetime burning in every moment / And not the lifetime of one man only / But of old stones that cannot be deciphered."

Henrion's twentieth solo exhibition expands upon the 80 year old artist's long-term project of "applying contemporary aesthetic sensibilities to traditional textile techniques and combining them with modern technologies." Like her other recent works, "Old Stones 3, (triptych)" was created by printing one of the her own digitally manipulated photographs on cotton fabric, then adding an intricate tactile quality to the surface via painstaking hand quilting with silk thread.

The central motif of the piece is a large crater filled with green grass, surrounded by stones and dry brush, seen within a panoramic landscape. Spanning all three panels, this manmade structure takes on the mysterious strangeness of a crop circle, dynamically achieving Henrion's stated aim of finding "resonance in the scientific theory of Complexity, as well as in poetry."

Henrion's hand-stitching, by the way, is never a random element in her work; for it invariably adds not only a sensuous "painterly" tactility to her pieces, but an underlying sense of depth, heft, and energy as well. The directions of the stitches and the patterns that they create vary greatly from one composition to another. In "Green Sea (triptych)," for example, where the entire composition is inspired by abstract patterns of flowing water and foam, the stitches form overlapping spirals that suggest the churning rhythms of ocean waves. By contrast in "Orange Sea (triptych)," where a beachscape and rolling surf spans all the three cotton scrolls, the stitches shower down in a slight vertical curve, like beams of light, complementing the golden auras which saturate the entire composition. The sun's reflection spreads and melts like an egg yolk on the surface of the water near the shoreline, where a tiny silhouetted human figure strolls and casts its shadow. Dwarfed like the travelers in classical Chinese landscapes by the magnitude of nature, this lone figure suggests our existential insignificance in relation to the natural wonders that surround us on our journey through life.

In a previous series, titled "Soft City," exhibited at Noho Gallery, and seen in part more recently at Highwire Gallery, in Philadelphia, Henrion focused on the storefronts and historic cast iron facades of New York's Soho art district. Whereas those compositions were architectonic, suggesting photorealist variations on Henrion's hardedge geometric abstract fiber art of past years, her present works evoke not only organic natural forms, but the vigorous gestural brushwork of Abstract Expressionism. This aspect of "Complexity" is especially striking in "Cornwall Rock (triptych)," where ruddy rocks and rushing blue water take on a gestural vivacity and a visceral, fleshy sensuality recalling de Kooning's nude bathers. Conversely, "Red Rock (triptych),"one of Henrion's boldest, most coloristically fiery large media pieces has an abstract angularity akin to Jack Tworkov coupled with a rugged cragginess reminiscent of Clyfford Still. Henrion, however, brings her own unique eloquence to this winning combination of attributes by virtue of the geological allusiveness she evokes through essentially nonobjective means.

In contrast to the expressionistic feeling of "Red Rock (triptych)," another large work called "Pink Rock (triptych) appears to reference Cubism, with its more subdued hues and depiction of flatter, more blocky rock formations, their fractured, shallow ridges hugging the picture plane for dear life. And in yet another large triptych titled "Gray Rock," Henrion appears to riff on Minimalism, with the more monolithic forms of monochromatic mineral surfaces presented in extreme close-up, with only their meticulously rendered shadows and striations serving as realist reference points.

Then there is "Lake Rock (triptych)," in which, without abandoning the underlying armature of abstraction that invariably bolsters even her most pictorial compositions, Henrion again ups the ante of representation. For here, with photorealist clarity, she conjures up a sparkling image of waves and rocks.

Although it is unusual for an artist who is as consummate a colorist as Marilyn Henrion to create major statements in monochromes, among the most striking compositions in the exhibition are two winter scenes that forsake her normally vibrant palette for grissaile. In "Chiaroscuro 1," delicate vertical water weeds are gracefully silhouetted against irregularly spaced horizontal stitches, suggesting ripples in a stream. In "Chiaroscuro 2," a structure suggesting the "Stairway to Heaven" in the famous Led Zeppelin song appears amid snow-laden branches in a forest. Both works find a mystery and a magic in natural settings that, were they alive today, Japanese master printmakers such as Hiroshige and Hokusai might have admired. And that Marilyn Henrion accomplishes this with a combination of state of the art technology and ancient textile techniques makes her own peculiar mastery all the more magical.

◊◊◊◊◊

Ed McCormack, a former columnist and feature reporter for Rolling Stone, and one of the original editors of Andy Warhol's Interview, has written extensively on art and popular culture for the Village Voice and numerous other publications. Presently, with his wife, Jeannie McCormack, he co-publishes the New York art journal Gallery & Studio.

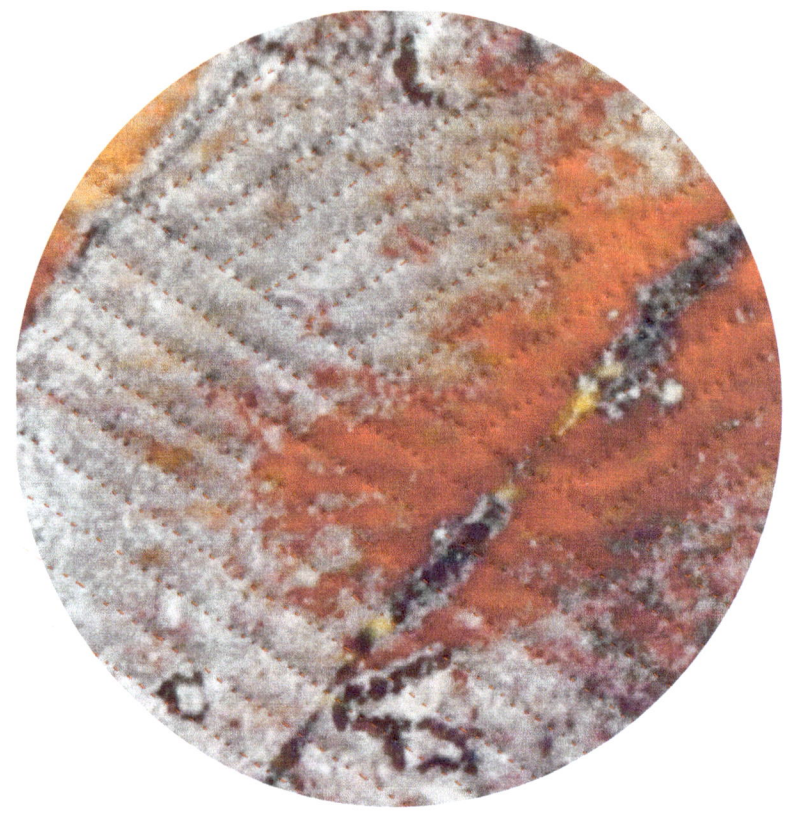

Red Rock triptych   50"x63"   Digitally manipulated photography, inkjet printing on cotton, hand stitching   2012

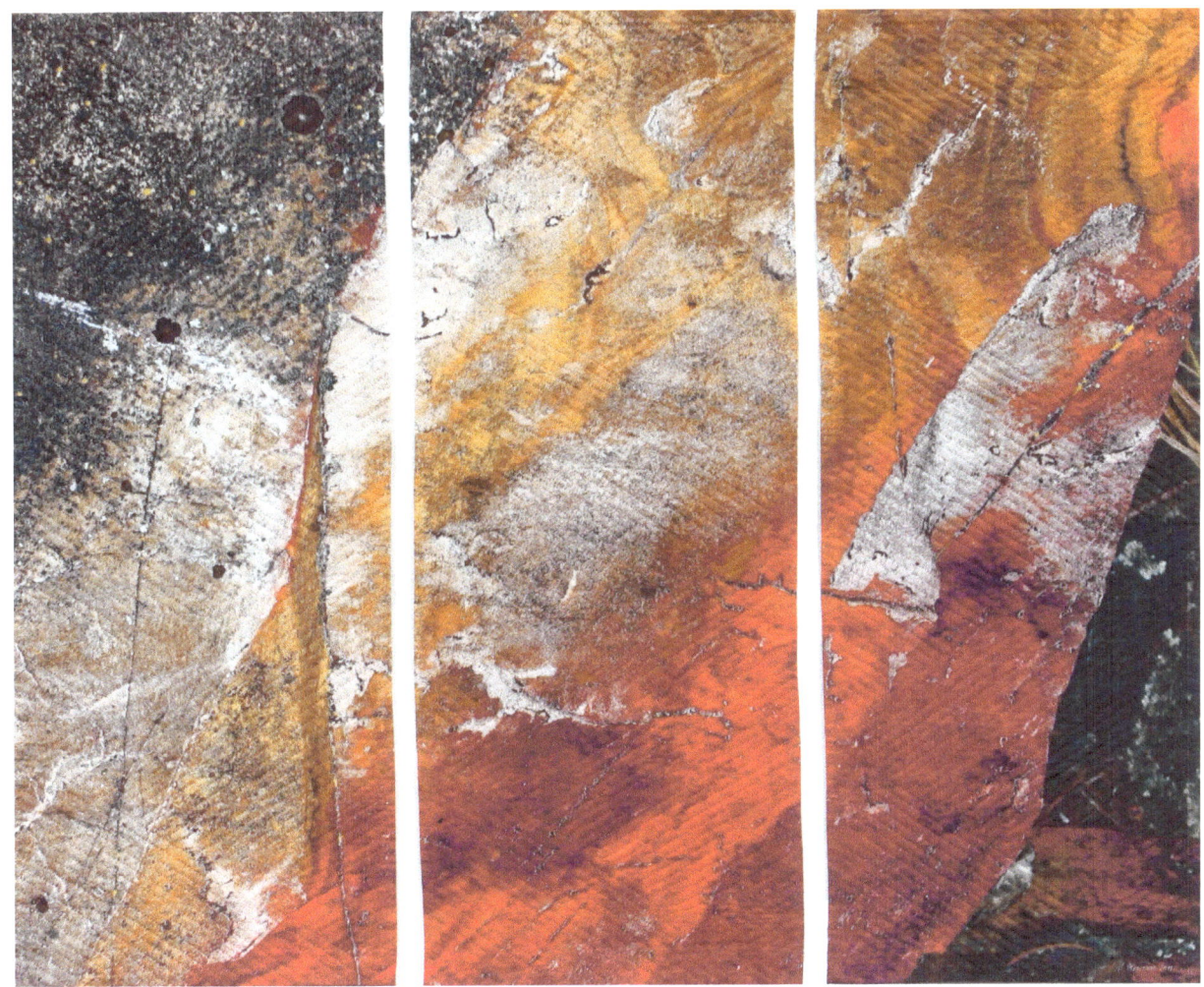

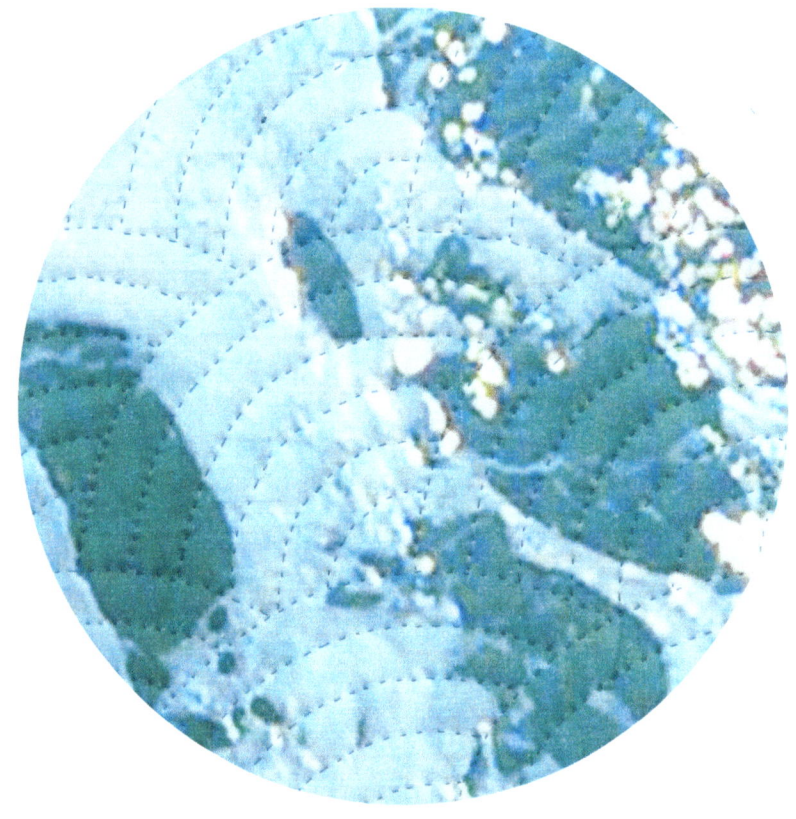

Green Sea triptych   50"x63"   Digitally manipulated photography, inkjet printing on cotton, hand stitching   2012

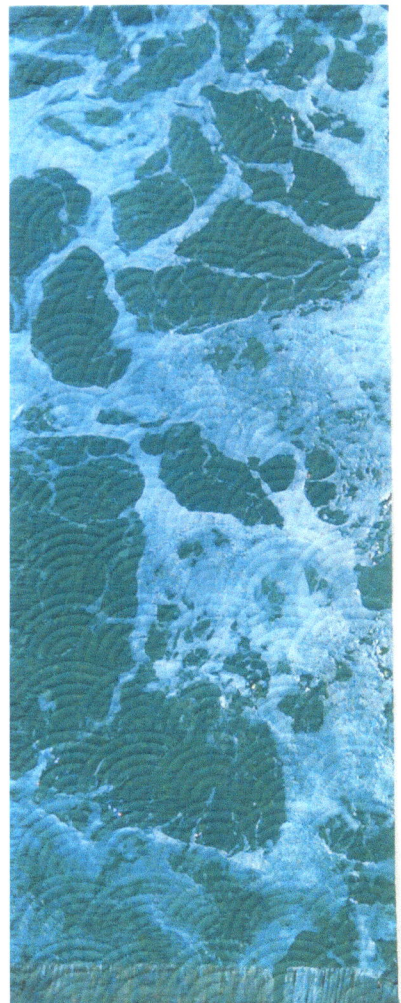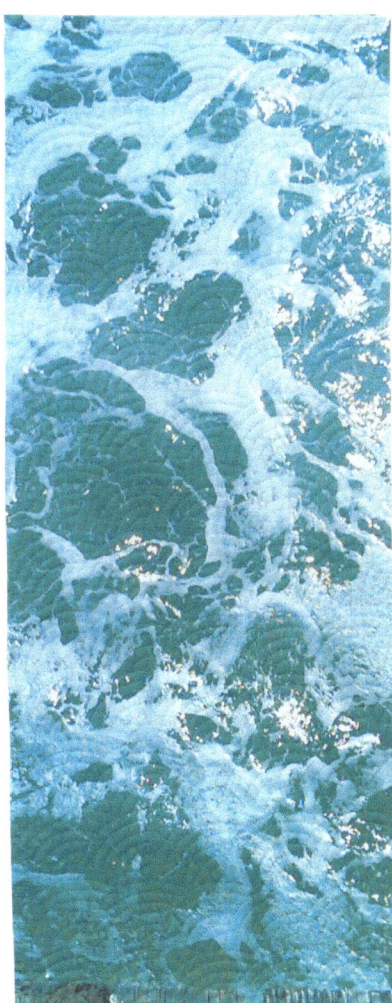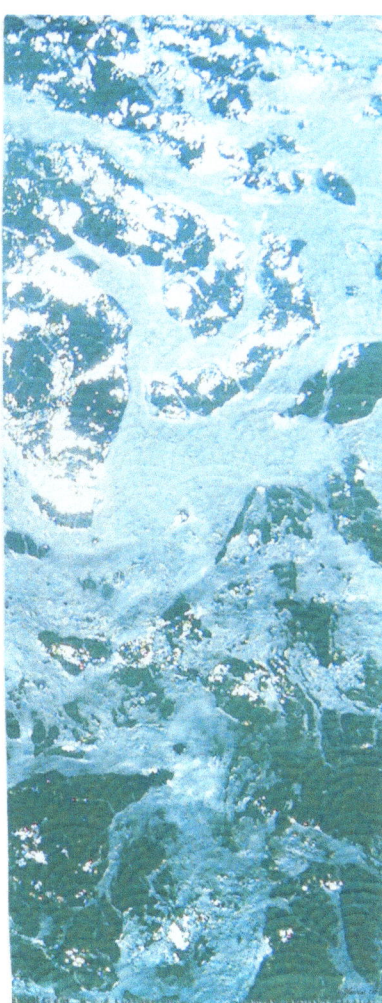

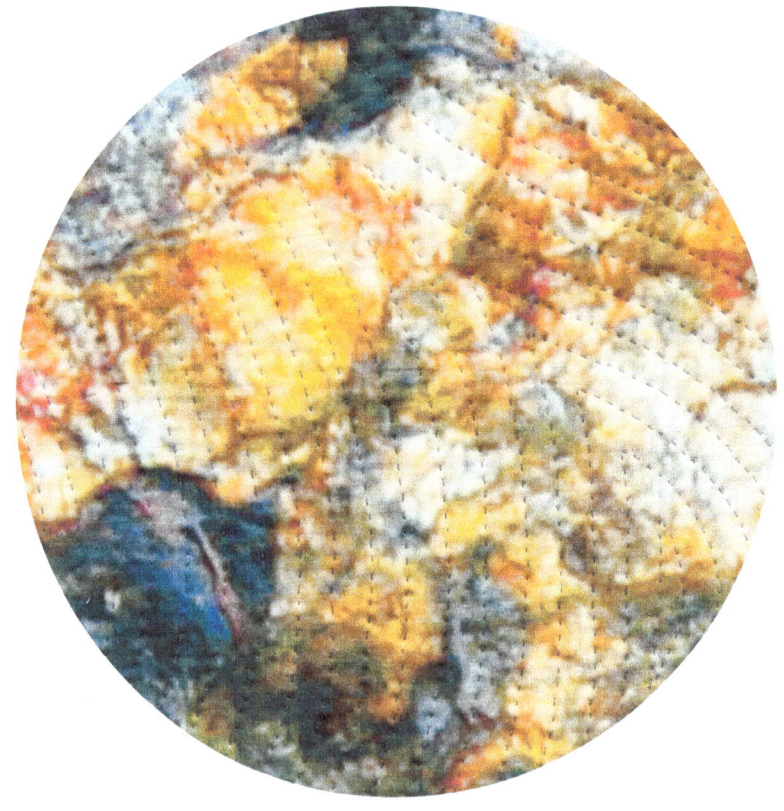

Cornwall Rock triptych 50"x63"   Digitally manipulated photography, inkjet printing on cotton, hand stitching   2012

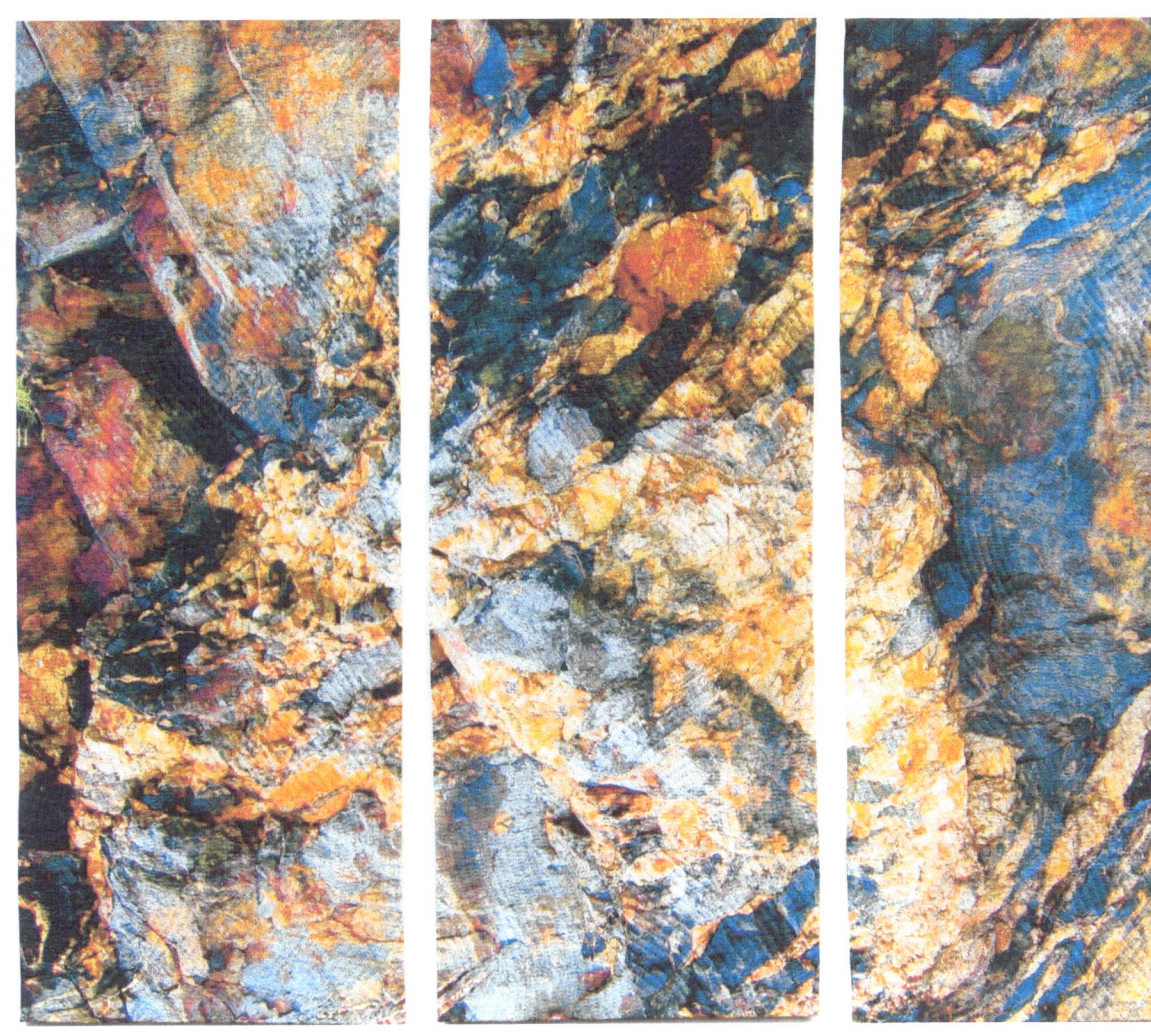

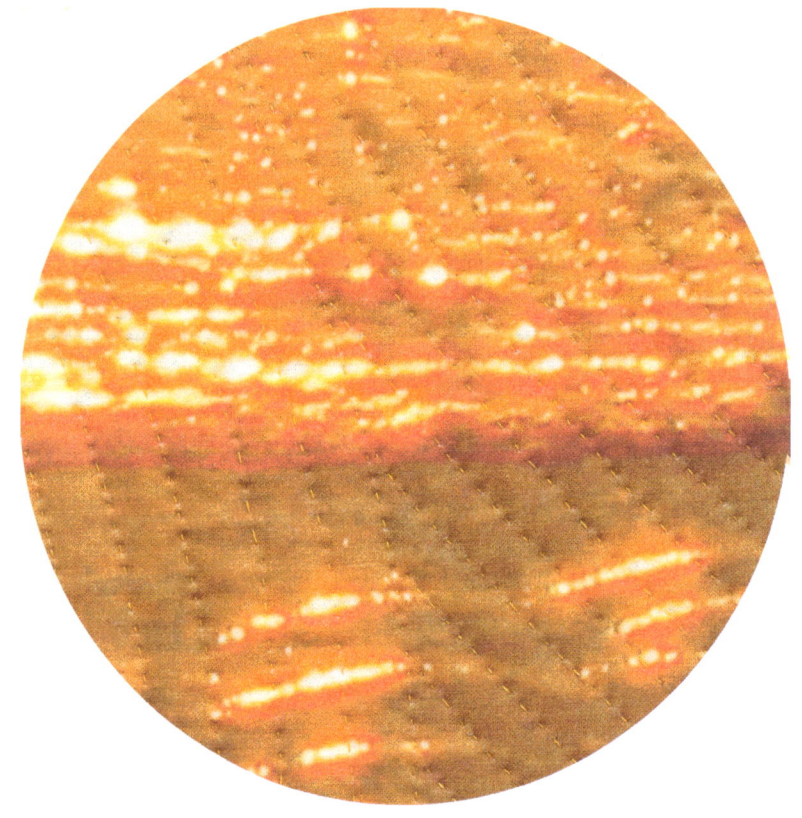

Orange Sea triptych   50"x63"   Digitally manipulated photography, inkjet printing on cotton, hand stitching   2012

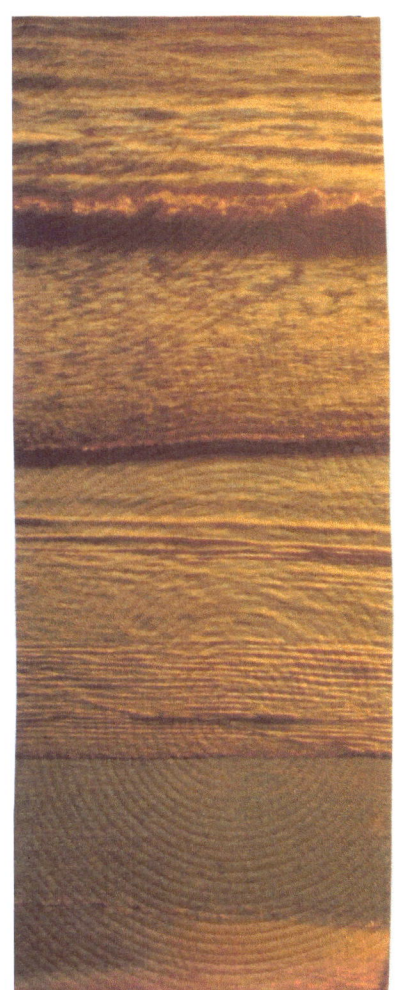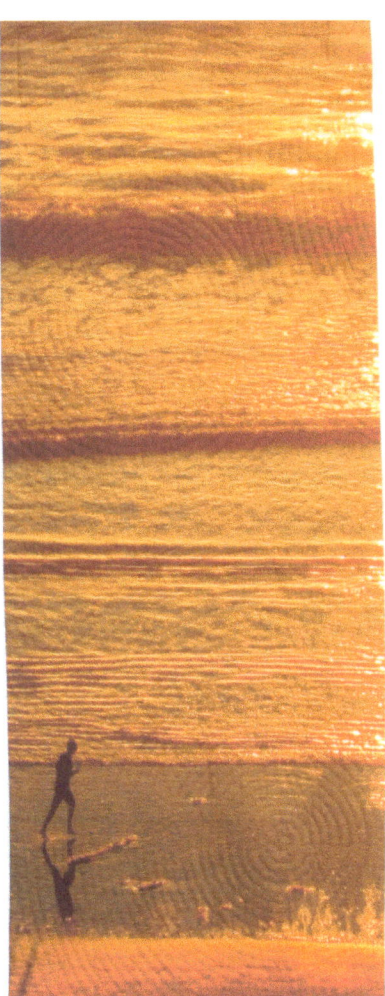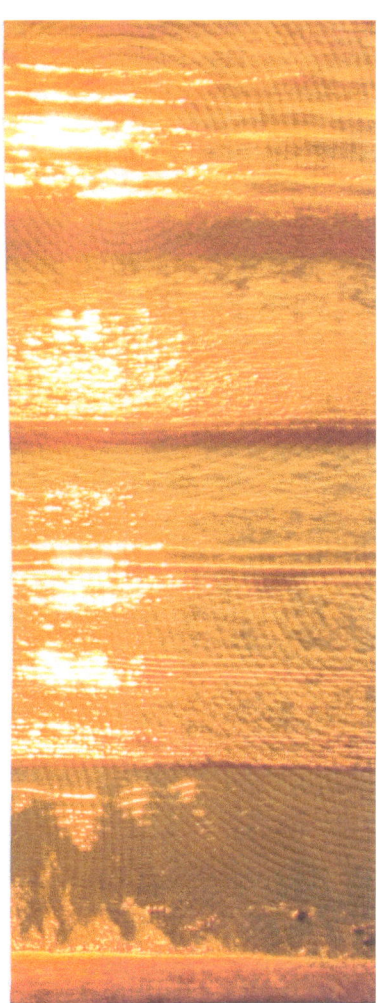

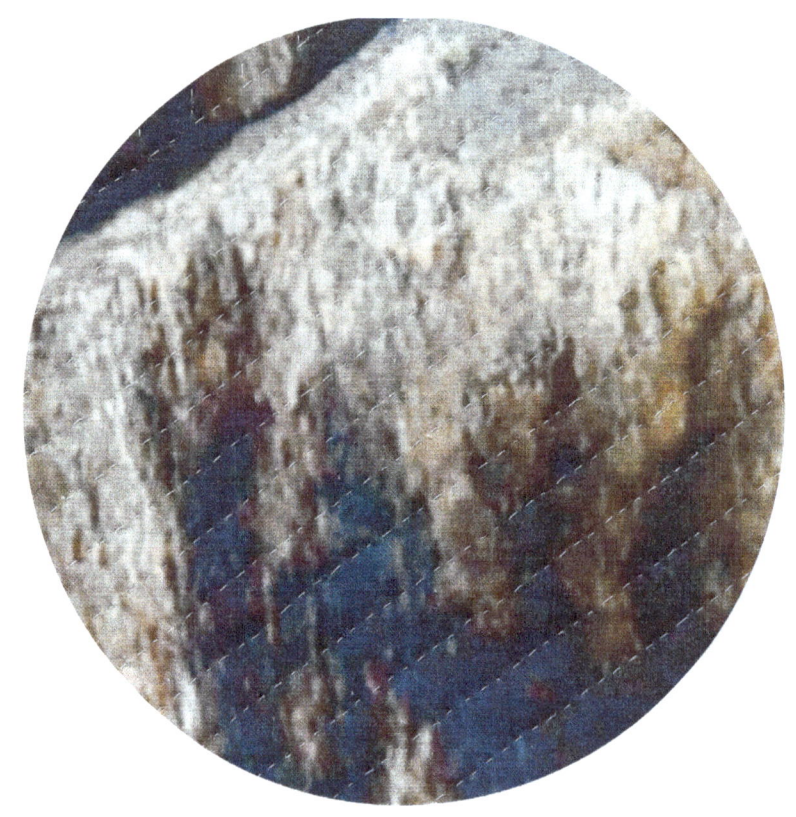

Gray Rock triptych 50"x63" Digitally manipulated photography, inkjet printing on cotton, hand stitching 2012

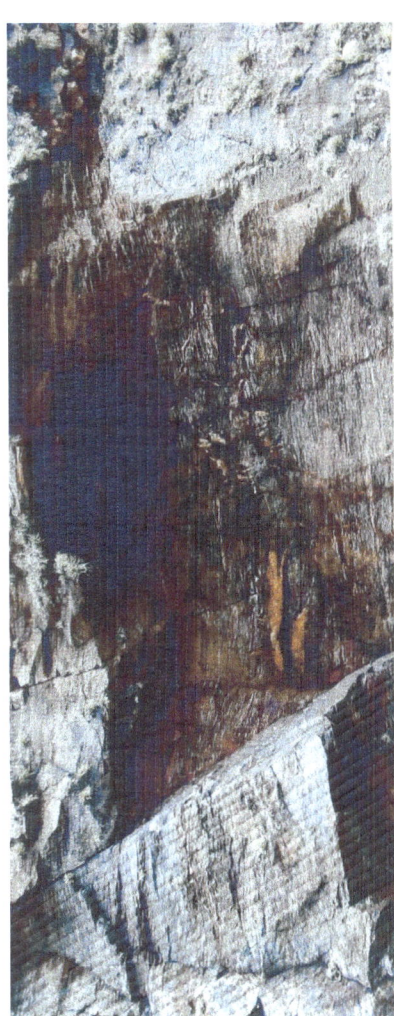 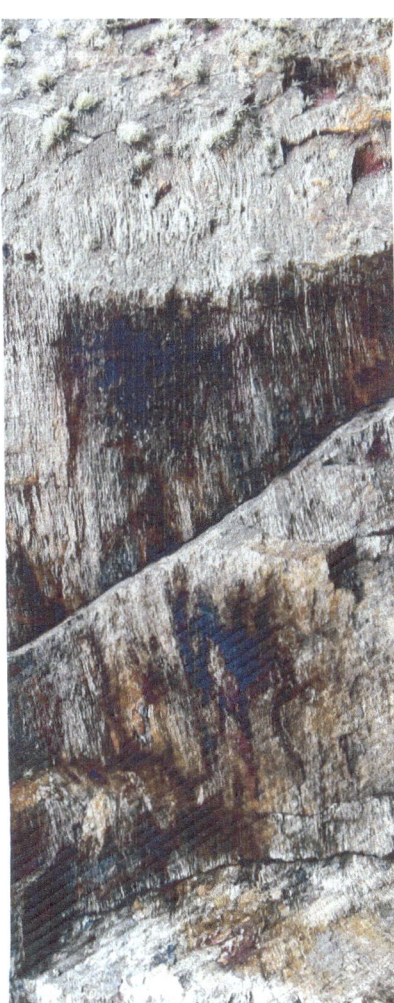 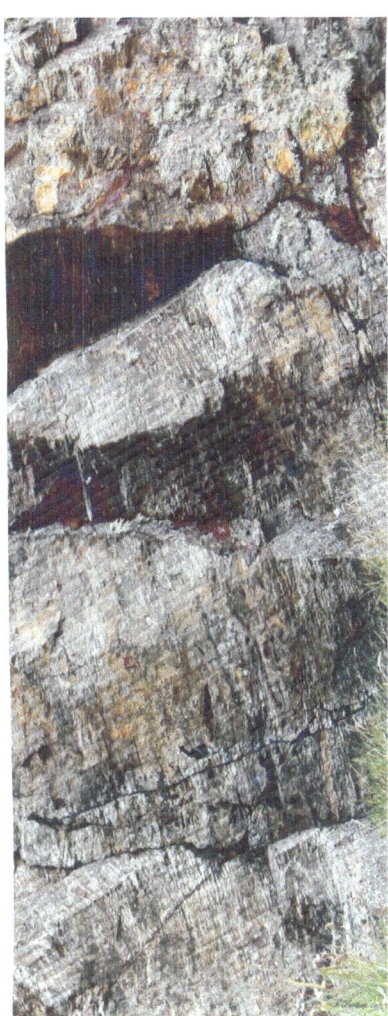

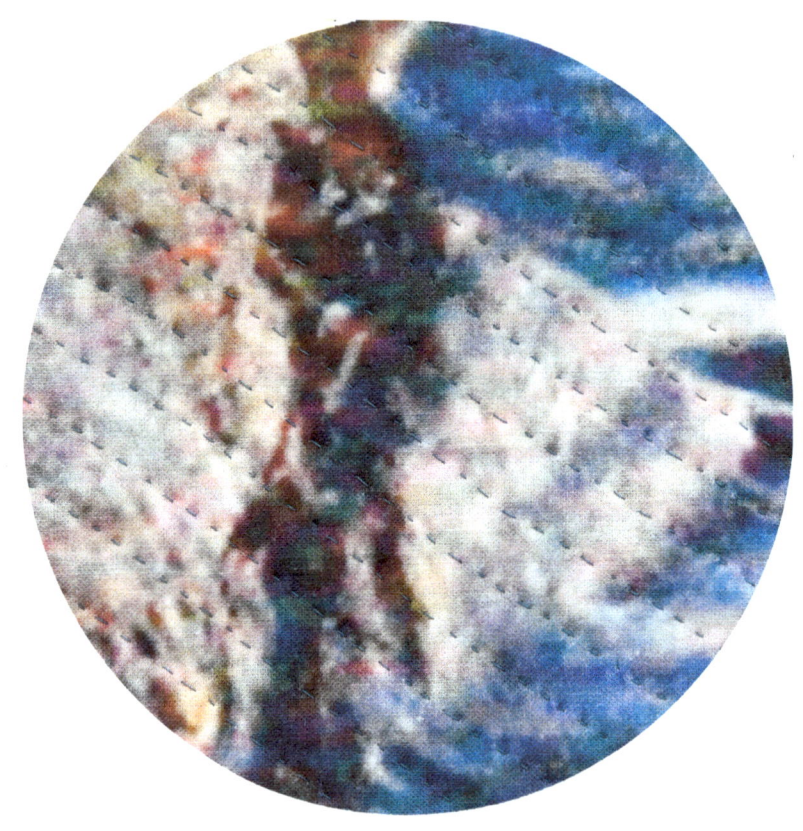

Lake Rock triptych   50"x63"   Digitally manipulated photography, inkjet printing on cotton, hand stitching   2012

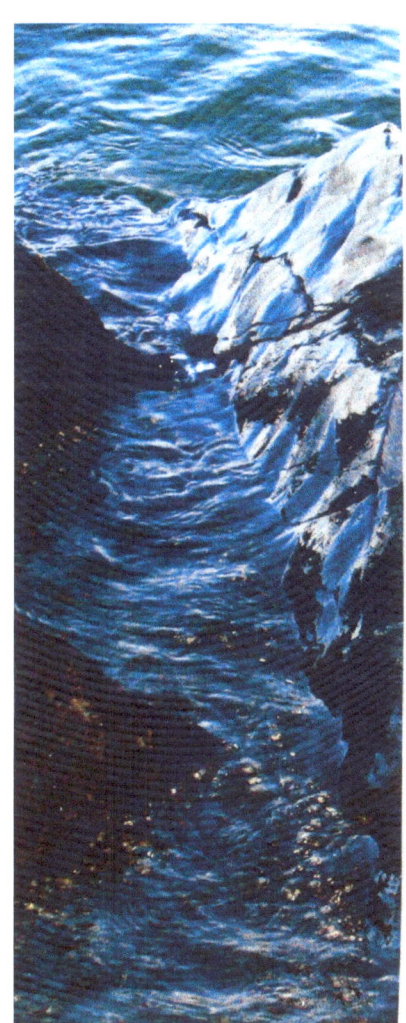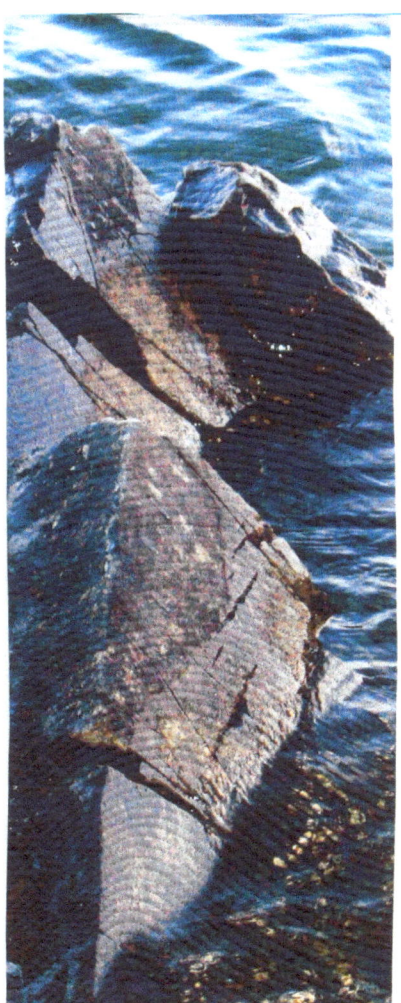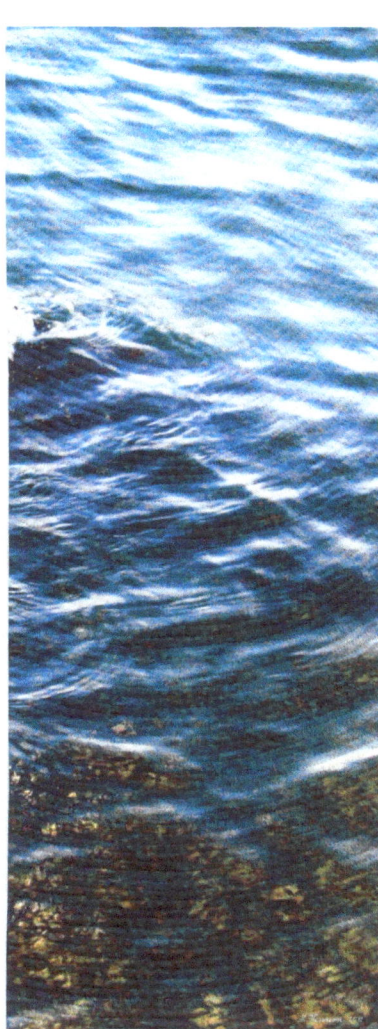

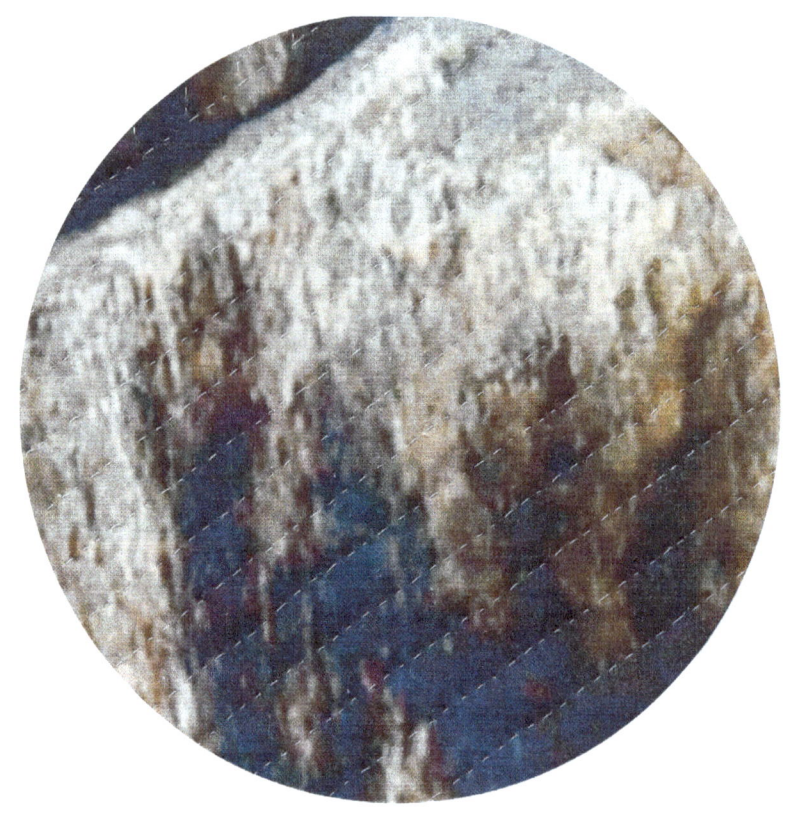

Pink Rock triptych   50"x63"   Digitally manipulated photography, inkjet printing on cotton, hand stitching   2012

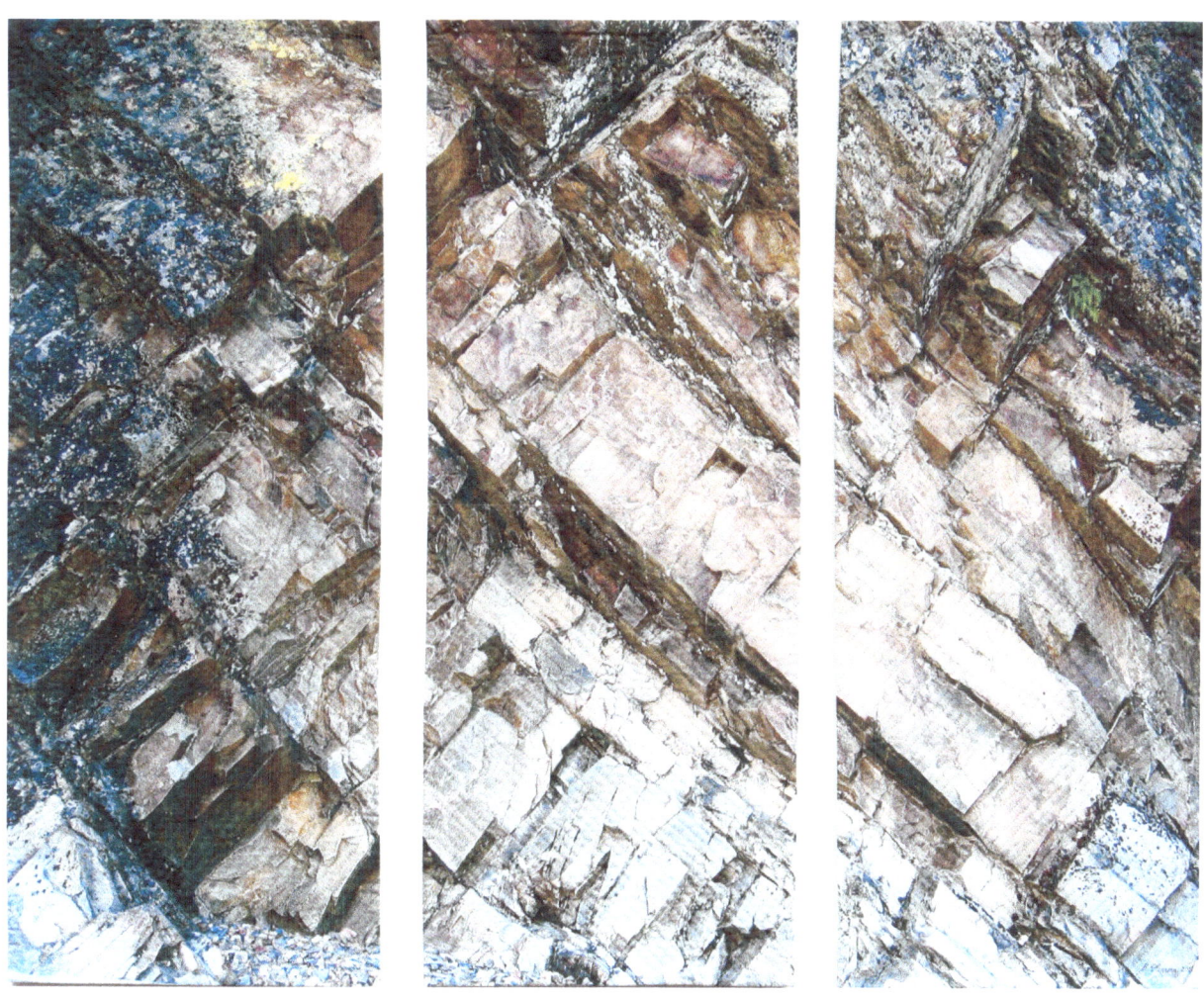

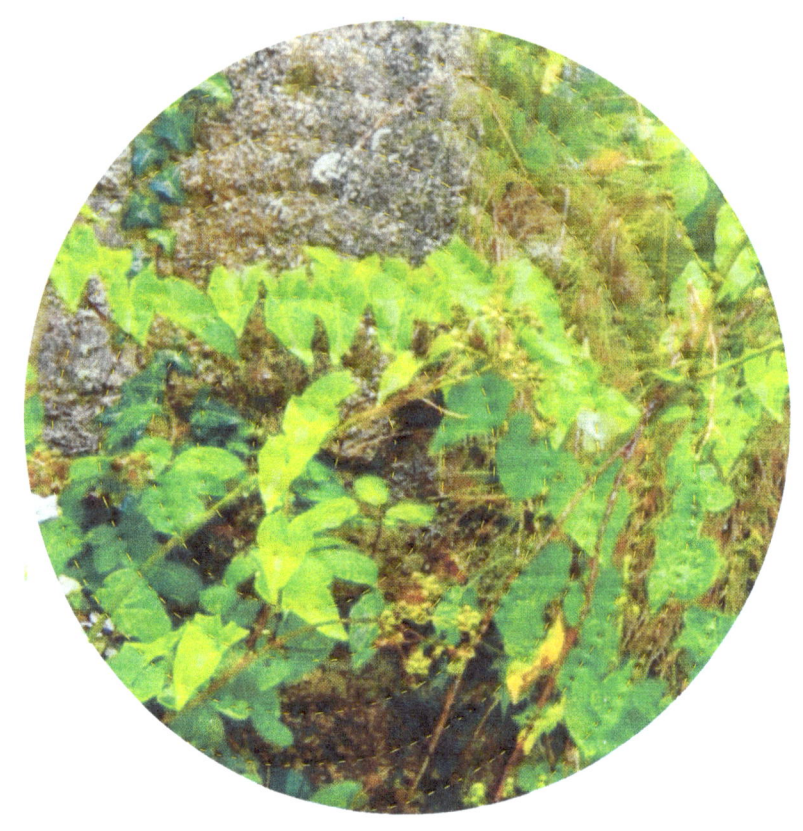

Old Stones 1   30"x25"   Digitally manipulated photography, inkjet printing on cotton, hand stitching   2012

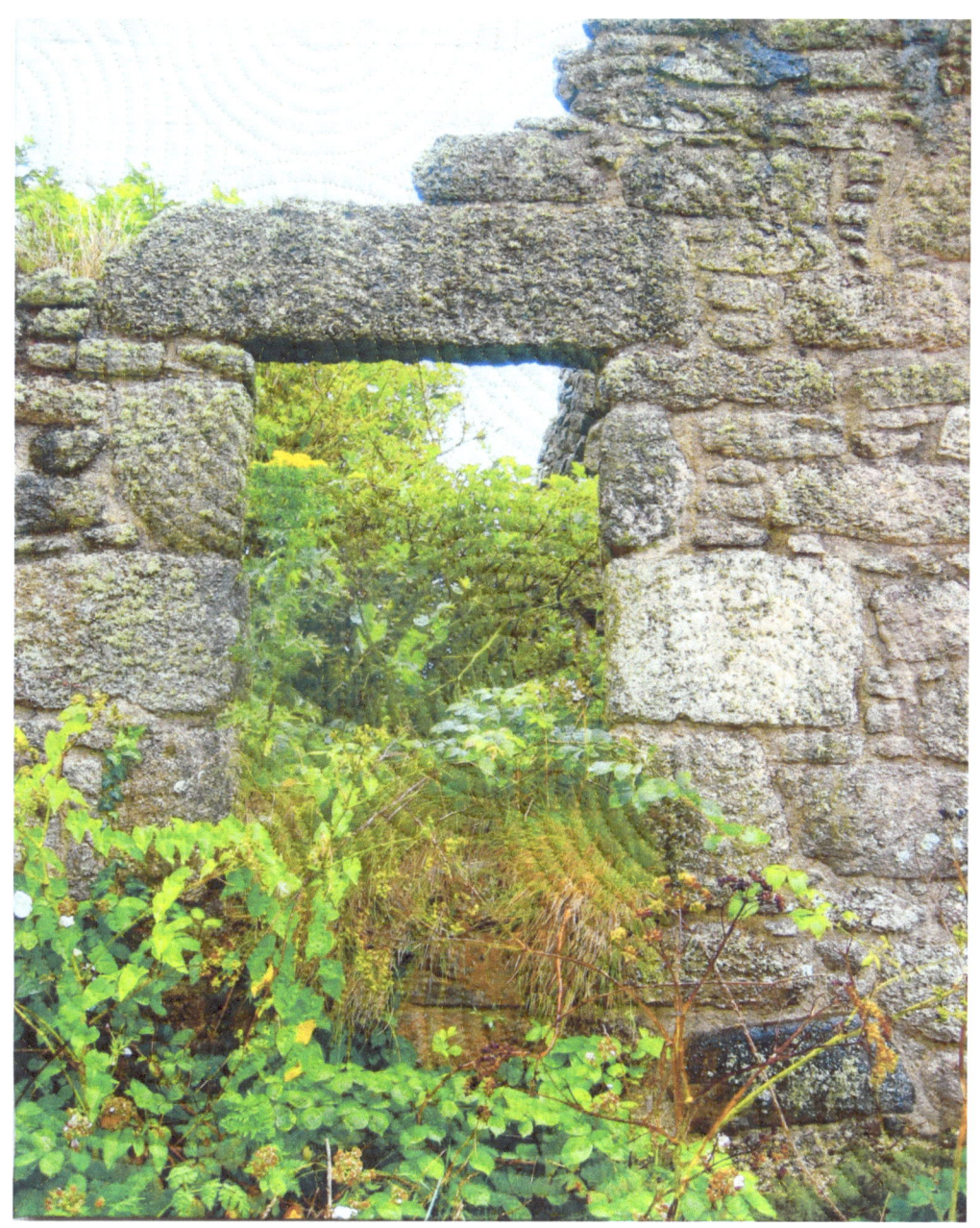

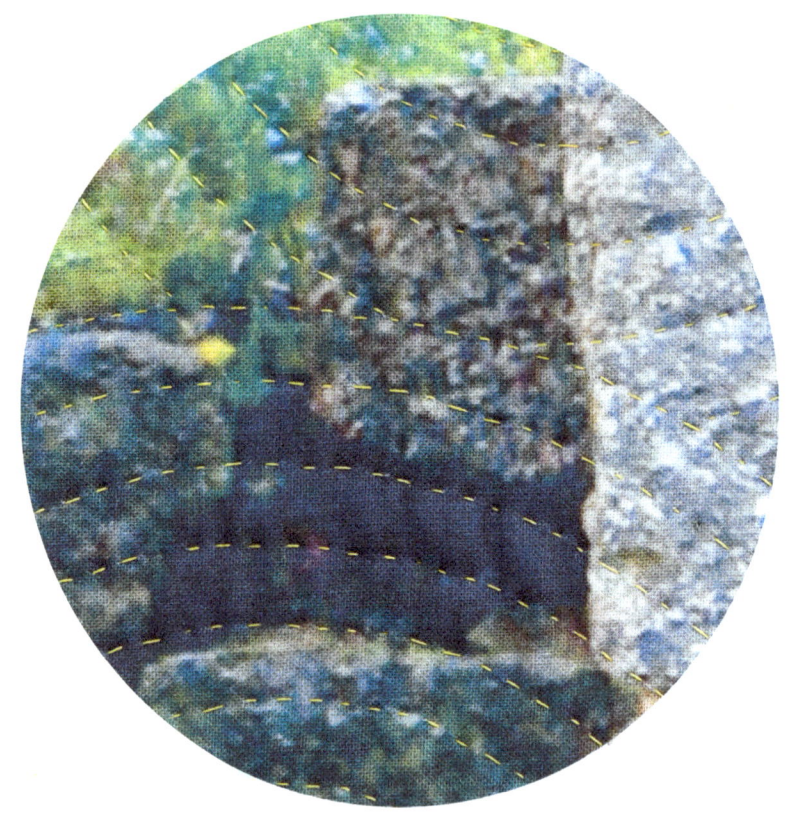

Old Stones 2   30"x25"   Digitally manipulated photography, inkjet printing on cotton, hand stitching   2012

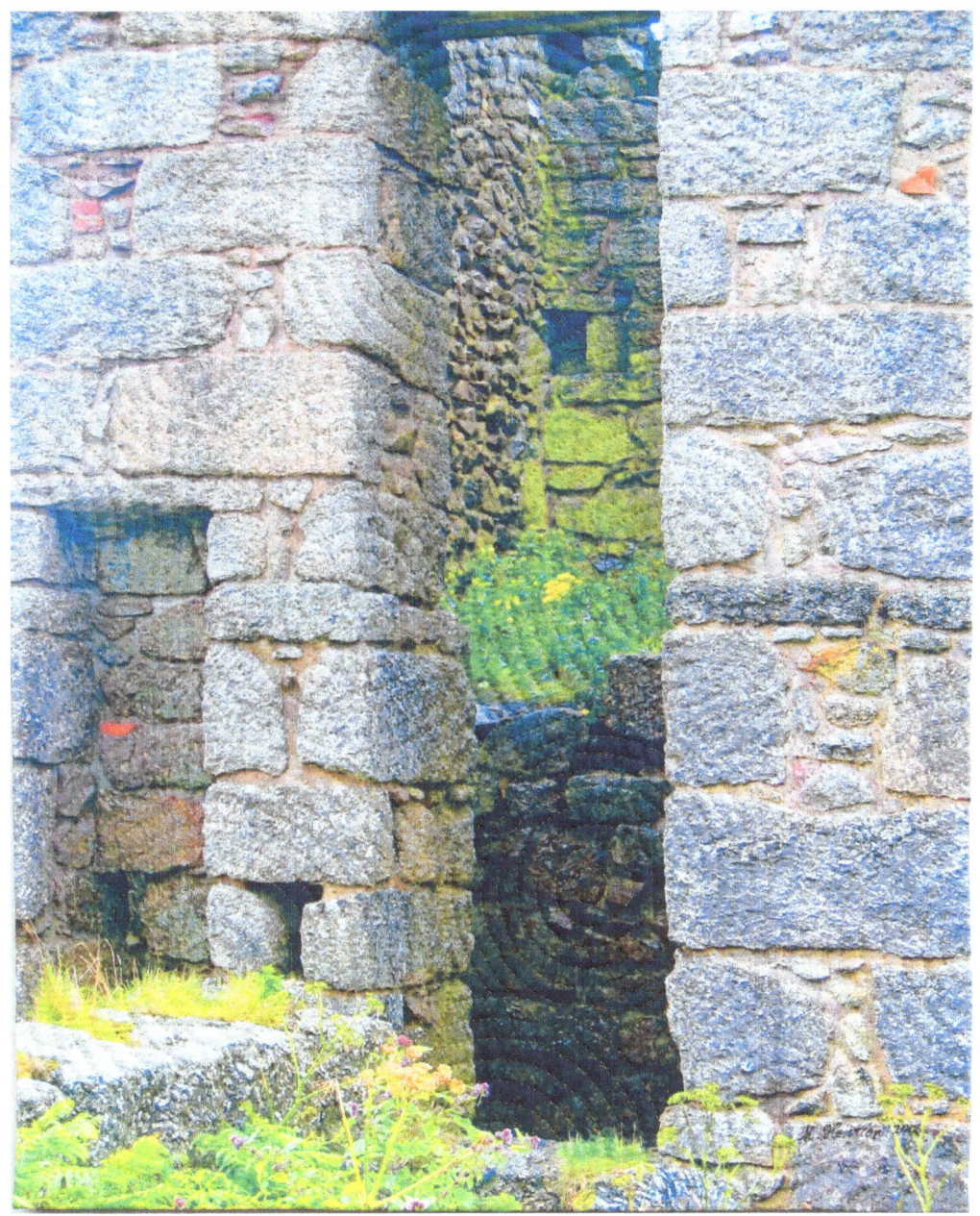

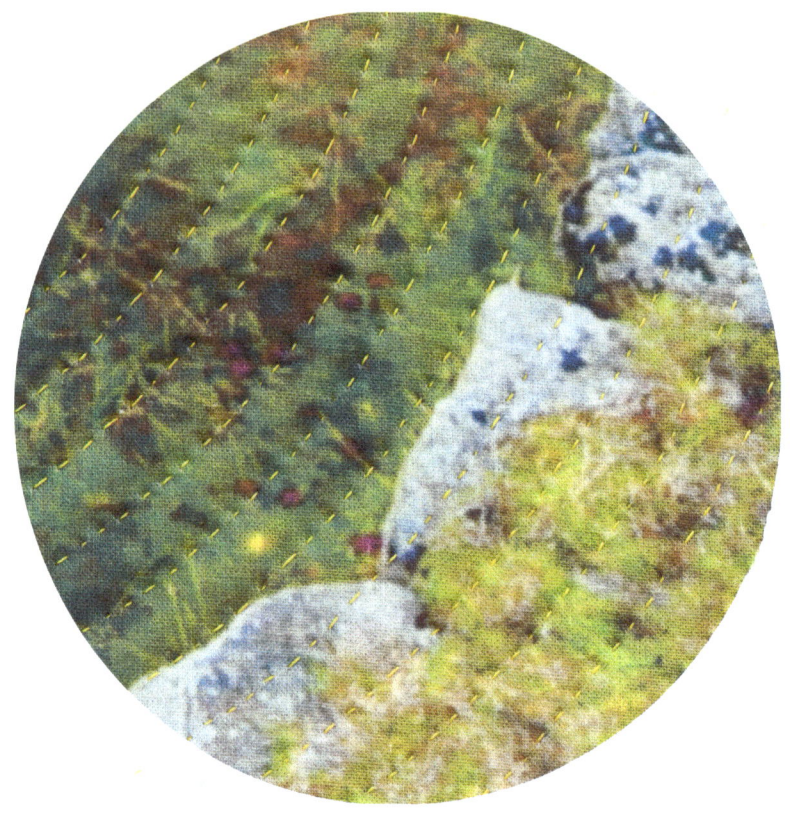

Old Stones 3 triptych   25""x32"   Digitally manipulated photography, inkjet printing on cotton, hand stitching   2012

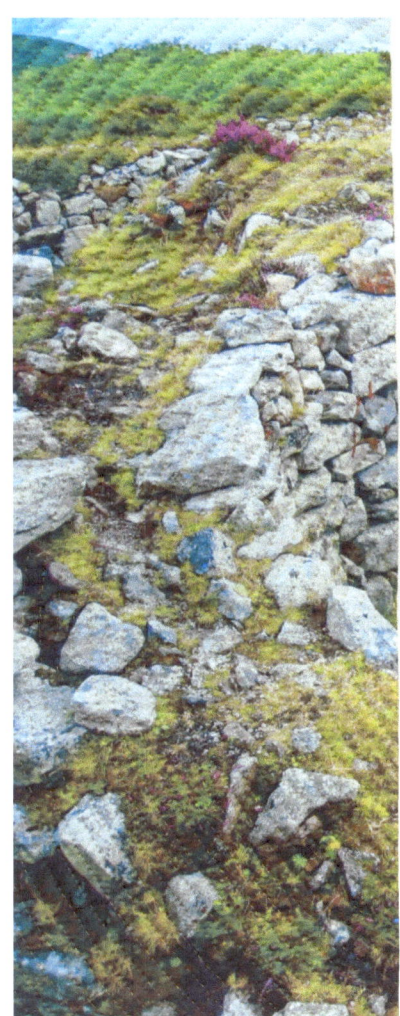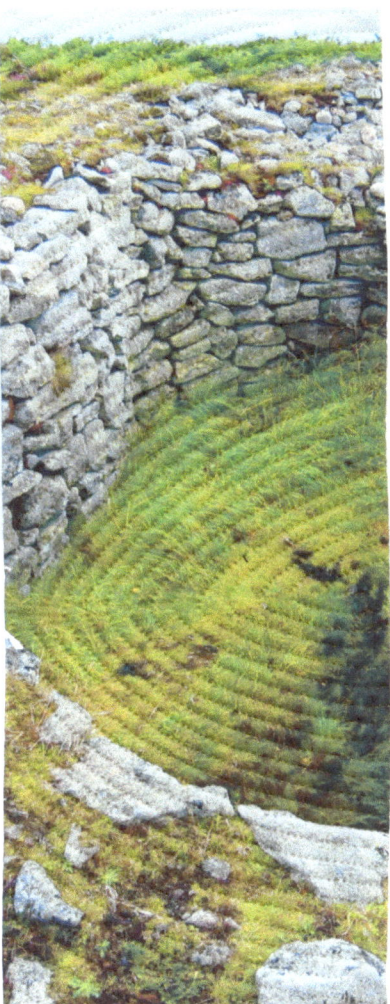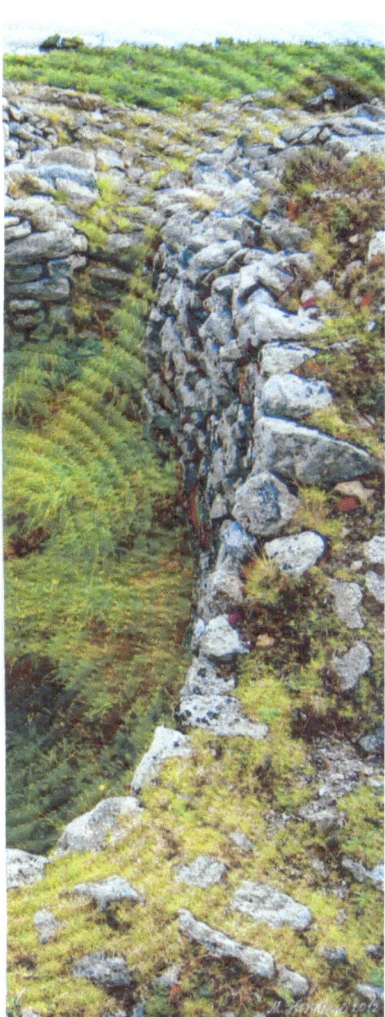

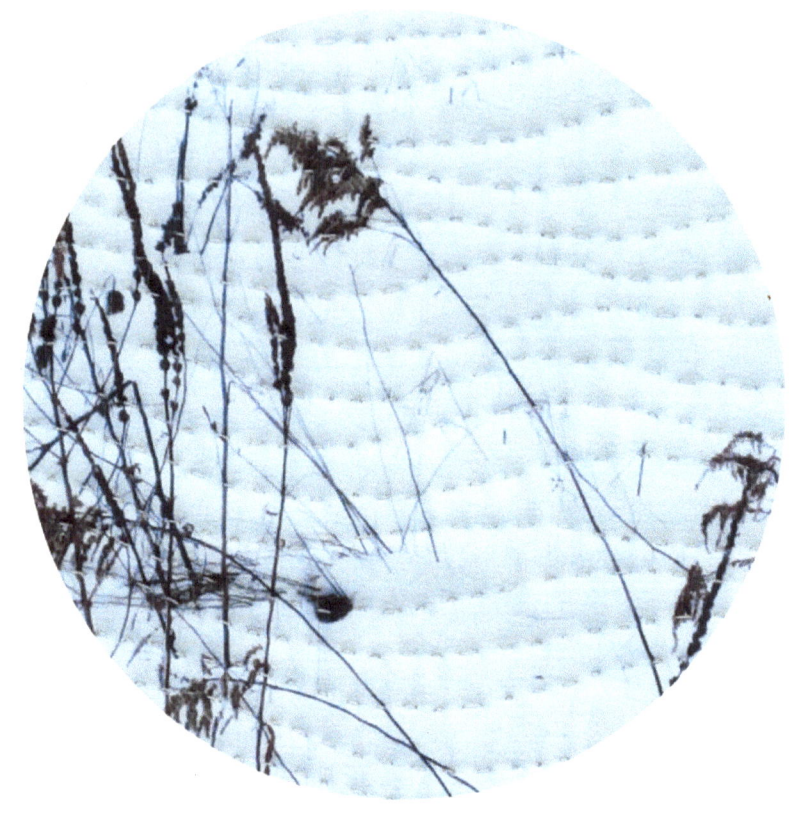

Chiarascuro 1   9.75"x7.5"   Digitally manipulated photography, inkjet printing on silk, hand stitching   2012

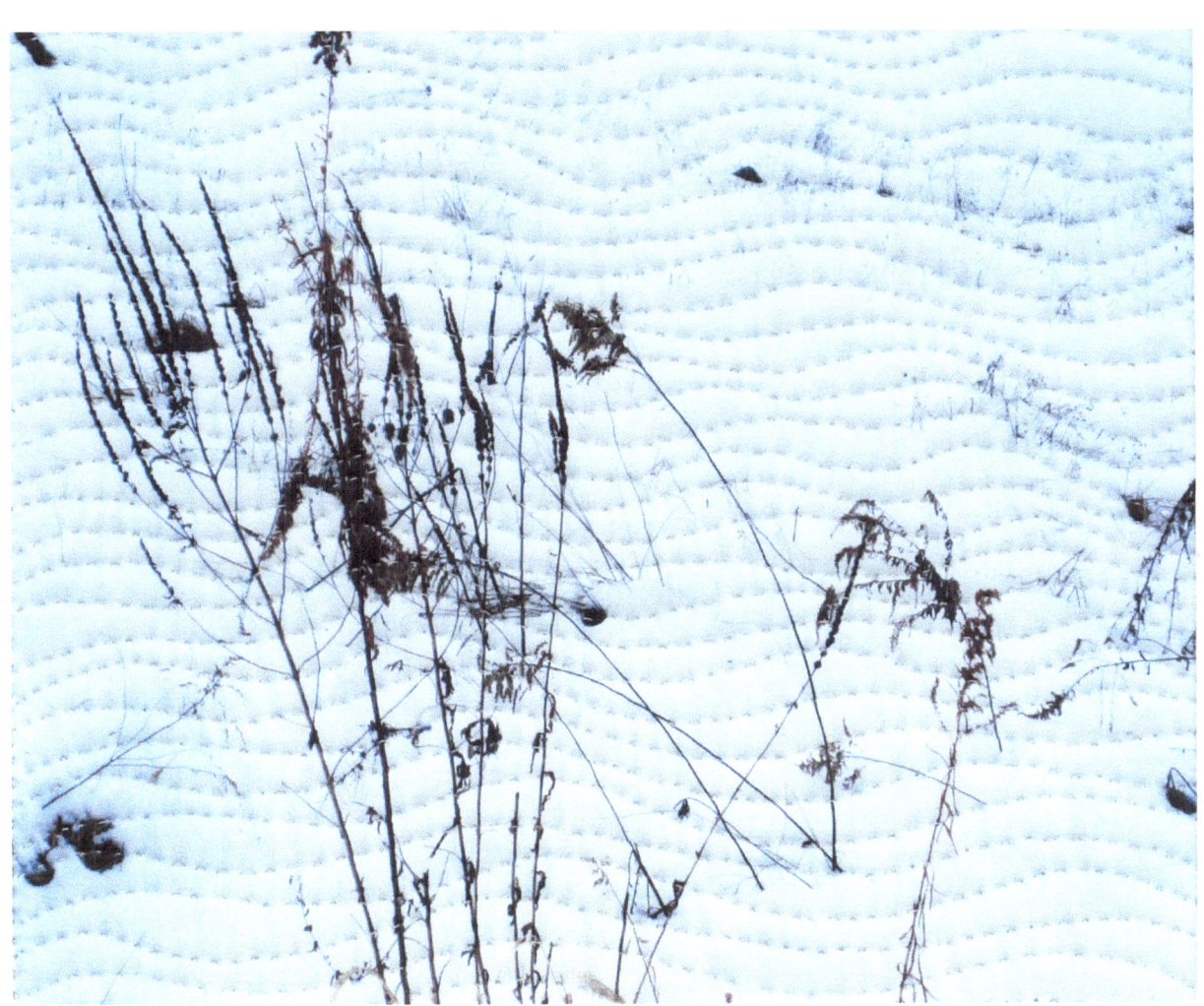

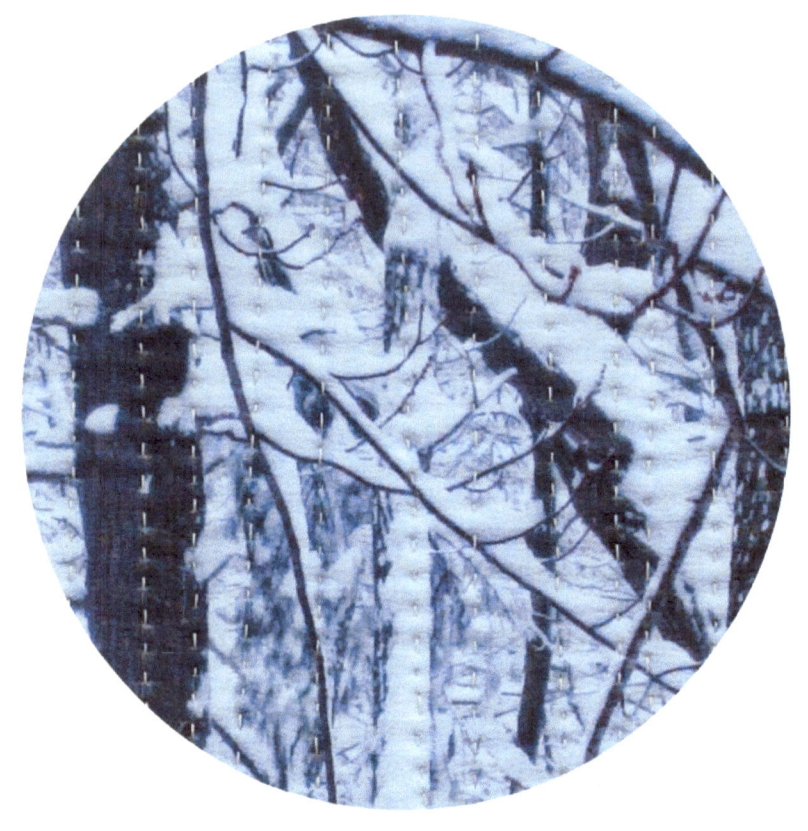

Chiarascuro 2   9.75"x7.5"   Digitally manipulated photography, inkjet printing on silk, hand stitching   2012

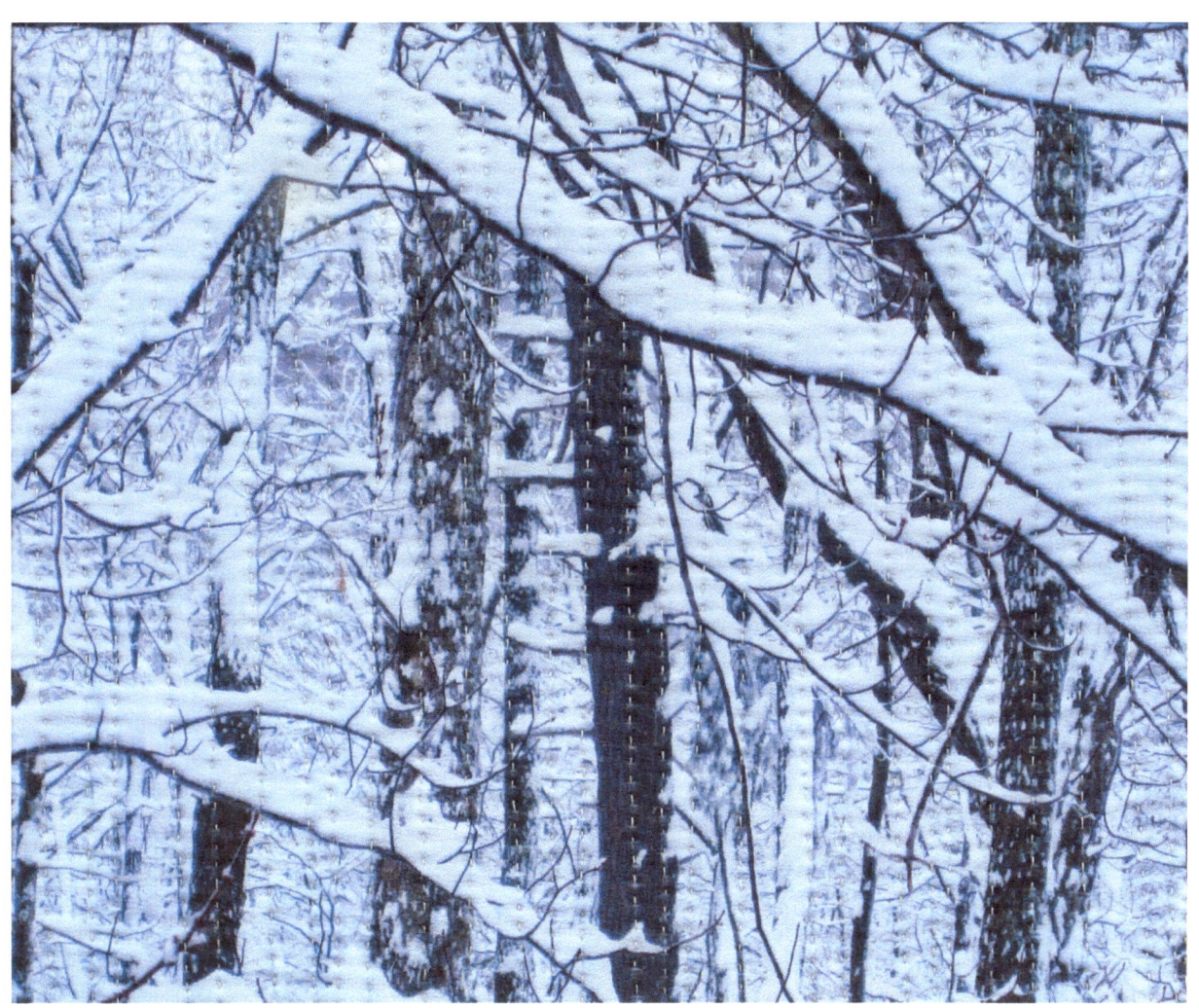

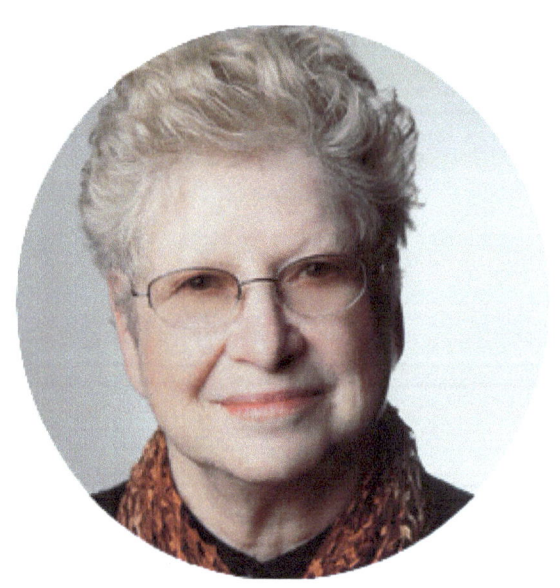

ABOUT THE ARTIST & HER WORK

A graduate of Cooper Union and a lifelong New Yorker, Marilyn Henrion is represented in the Smithsonian Institution's Archives of American Art in Washington, DC. Her award winning artworks have been exhibited in museums and galleries worldwide. They are in major museum, corporate and private collections, including the Museum of Arts & Design in New York, the Newark Museum, Newark, NJ, the National Quilt Museum, Paducah, KY, the International Quilt Museum, Lincoln, NE, and the U.S. State Department Embassy in Pnom Penh, Cambodia. They have also been featured in numerous publications including "Women Designers in the U.S.-1900-2000" Yale University Press, "Fiber Art Today" by Carol K. Russell, and "Contemporary Quilt Art" by Kate Lenkowsky,

Among the grants Henrion has received was one awarded by the Artslink Partnership, devoted to fostering excellence in the arts between the U.S. and countries of the former Soviet Union. In 2005, she was awarded a fellowship by the New York Foundation for the Arts.

This latest series of works, introduced at Noho Gallery in New York in April, 2012. marks her 20th solo exhibition and her 80th birthday.

CURRICULUM VITAE

Selected Solo Exhibitions

2012   Noho Gallery, New York, NY

2010   Visions Art Museum, San Diego, CA
        Noho Gallery, New York, NY

2009   Bayer Corporation, Wayne & Montvale, NJ
        Berkeley College Art Gallery, New York, NY

2008   Noho Gallery, New York, NY

2006   Noho Gallery, New York, NY
        Galerie Gora, Montreal, Quebec, Canada

2005   Treasure Room Gallery,, New York, NY

2004   Noho Gallery, New York, NY

2002   Noho Gallery, New York, NY

2001   Thirteen Moons Gallery, Santa Fe, NM

2000   Noho Gallery, New York, NY

1997   Decouvrir Gallery, Seattle, WA
        La Conner Quilt Museum, La Conner, WA
        Atlantic Comm.College Art Gallery, NJ
        Leman Publications Art Gallery, Golden, CO

1996   American Assoc. for the Advancement of Science,
        Washington, DC

1994   Merrill Lynch Corporate Headquarters,
        Plainsboro, NJ

1992   Educational Testing Services Corp.,
        Princeton,NJ

Selected Group Exhibitions

2012   Highwire Gallery, Philadelphia, PA

2011   World Financial Center Gallery, NY, NY
        National Quilt Museum, Paducah, KY

2011   NYIT School of Architecture & Design
        New Arts Center, Lancaster, PA
        Lehman College Art Gallery, Bx, NY
        Rochester Contemp. Arts Center., Rochester, NY

2010   Morris Museum, Morristown, NJ
        Betty Dare Gallery, Chicago, IL
        Osilas Gallery, Bronxville, NY

2009   Museum of Arts & Design, NY, NY
        Natl. Taiwan Living Arts Center, Taiwan City,
         Taiwan
        Coos Art Museum, Coos Bay, OR
        Binghamton Univ. Art Museum, Binghamton, NY
        Columbus Cultural Arts Center, Columbus, OH
        The Williams Club, NY, NY

2008   Columbus Art Museum, Columbus, OH
        Monmouth Museum, Lincoln, NJ
        Comma Gallery, Orlando, FL
        Peabody Auditorium Gallery, Daytona Beach, FL

2007   Lincoln Center Galleries, Ft. Collins, CO
        Pen & Brush Gallery, NY, NY
        Fieldstone Fine Art Gallery, Ramsey, NJ
        John Michael Kohler Artspace, Sheboygin, WI

2006   Ross Art Museum, Delaware, OH
        Chandler Arts Center, Chandler, AZ
        Klein Art Gallery, Philadelohia, PA

2005   Carl Solway Gallery, Cincinatti, OH
        Center for Visual Arts, Denton, TX
        Sweeney Arts Center, Santa Fe, NM
        Fitton Arts Center, Hamilton, OH

2004   American Textile History Museum, Lowell, MA
        Arkansas Historic Museum, Little Rock, AR

2003 Birmingham Bloomfield Arts Cntr., Birmingham, MI
Paine Arts Center, Oshkosh, WI
Johnson Humrickhouse Museum, Coshocton, OH

2002 Albright Knox Museum Gallery, Buffalo, NY
UBS Paine Webber Galleries, NY, NY
Thirteen Moons Gallery, Santa Fe, NM

2001 Longview Art Museum, Longview, TX
Nabisco Corp. Art Gallery, E. Hanover, NJ
Dairy Barn Cultural arts Center, Athens, OH
Fort Smith Civic Center, Fort Smith, AR

2000 Bard Graduate Center Gallery, NY, NY
Rotunda Gallery, NM State Capitol, Santa Fe, NM
Pavillion Josephine, Strasbourg, France
Leslie Powell Foundation Gallery, Lawton, OK

1999 New York State Museum, Albany, NY
Cornell Museum, Delray Beach, FL
American Craft Museum, NY, NY
J.C. Epstein Museum Gallery, W. Bloomfield, MI
Sedgwick Cultural Center, Philadelphia, PA

1998 Tokyo International Forum, Tokyo, Japan
Museum of San Diego History, San Diego, CA
Firelands Assoc. for the Visual Arts, Oberlin, OH

1997 Islip Art Museum, Islip, NY
N. Y. State Museum, Albany, NY
Gross McCleaf Gallery, Philadelphia, PA

1996 Museum of Decorative & Applied Arts, Moscow, Russia
The Museum at Stony Brook, Stony Brook, NY
Hoyt Institute of Fine Arts, New Castle, PA
Arthur Houghton Art Gallery, Cooper Union, NY

1995 Museum of American Quilters, Paducah, KY

1995 Gross McCleaf Gallery, Philadelphia, PA

994 James A. Michener Art Museum, Doylestown, PA

1999 Oklahoma City Art Museum, Oklahoma City, OK
Yeshiva University Museum, New York, NY
NASA Ames Research Center, Mountain View, CA

1993 Museum of Decorative & Applied Arts, Moscow, Russia
J.C. Epstein Museum Gallery, Bloomfield, MI

1992 La Bibliotheque Fornay, l'hotel de Sens, Paris, France
Decatur House, Washington, DC
The Museum at Stony Brook, Stony Brook, NY

1991 New York City Cultural Affairs Gallery, N.Y., NY
Schweinfurth Art Center, Auburn, NY

1990 Fuji Bank, N. Y., NY

Selected Collections

Museum of Arts & Design, New York, NY
Newark Museum, Newark, NJ
International Quilt Study Center Museum, Lincoln, NE
National Quilt Museum, Paducah, KY
U.S. State Dept., U.S. Embasyy, Pnom Penh, Cambodia
Lucent Technologies, Denver, CO
Avaya Corporation, Denver, CO
Kaiser Permanente, Denver, CO
Dana Farber Cancer institute, Boston, MA
Comanche County Medical Center, Lawton, OK
Carnegie Abbey Country Club, Naragansett, RI
SAS Institute, Cary, NC
Rodale Press, Emmaus, PA
Nihon Vogue, Tokyo, Japan
Valley Hospital, Ridgewood, NJ
Santa Rita Medical Center, Lima, OH

Selected Honors & Awards

2005   New York Foundation for the Arts Fellowship

2003   Brisons Veor Trust, Artist Residency Fellowship, Cornwall, England

2002   Invited by Smithsonian Institution's Archives of American Art to donate all personal and professional documents and sketchbooks for the permanent collection.

1999   New York State Craft alliance Grant

1997   Friends of Fiber art International Grant

1996   Nihon Vogue Grant

1995/6   Artslink Partnership Grant (National Endowment for the Arts & The Open Society funding)

Selected Bibliography

"Fiber Art Today" by Carol K. Russell, Schiffer Publishing, Atglen, PA, May, 2011

"Patchwork City", by Patty Lee, New York Daily News, Sunday Nov. 14, 2010 (double page centerfold)

"Soft City: Marilyn Henrion", exhibition catalog with essay by Ed McCormack, November, 2010

"Noise: New Works by Marilyn Henrion", Jacqueline Ruyak, Surface Design Journal, Summer 2009

"Marilyn Henrion: Making Noise", Sandra Sider, Fiberarts Magazine, February, 2009

"Marilyn Henrion: Noise", Exhibition catalog with essays by Janet Koplos & Ed McCormack

"Materials, Innovation Matter", Bill Mayr, The Columbus Dispatch, June 15, 2008

"Contemporary Quilt Art", Kate Lenkowsky, Indiana University Press, 2008

"Quilting Transformed:Leaders In Contemporary Quilting in the United States-The 20th Century and Beyond",

"Shared Threads", Jacqueline Atkins, Nihon Vogue Co. Ltd., Tokyo, Japan, 2007

"Marilyn Henrion: Disturbances", exhibition catalog, 2006

"Geometry Unmoored", Ed McCormack, Gallery & Studio, September, 2006

"Inner and Outer Horizons in the Art of Marilyn Henrion", Ed McCormack, Gallery & Studio, June,2004

"Marilyn Henrion: On Building Careers", Patricia Malarcher, Surface Design Journal, Winter 2004

"Inspiration", U.S. Embassy in Gaborone, Art In Embassies Program, U.S. Dept. of State, Nov., 2003

"Marilyn Henrion's Ultimate Triumph", Ed McCormack, Gallery & Studio, Nov/Dec 2002/Jan 2003

"Folk-Art Aesthetics and American Art Quilts, Sandra Sider, FIBERARTS, Nov./Dec., 2003

"Marilyn Henrion at Noho Gallery", Raymond J. Steiner, Art Times Journal, January, 2003

"Quilts From Six Continents: The American Craft Museum Collection", Catalog Essay by Curator, Ursula Neuman, 2002

"The Best Contemporary Quilts", Lark Books, 2001

"Women Designers in the U.S.A.-1900-2000", Dr. Pat Kirkham, Yale University Press, Nov., 2000

"Marilyn Henrion's Commanding Colors", FIBERARTS, March/April, 2001
"Marilyn Henrion at Noho",Surface Design Journal,Winter,2001
"Tradition & Innovation In The Art of Marilyn Henrion", Gallery & Studio, June/July, 2000
"Cloth Poems: Art Quilts by Marilyn Henrion, Art Quilt Magazine # 9, 1998
"The Art Quilt" by Robert Shaw, pub.Hugh Lauter Levin, 1997
"Geometrie et Sensibilitie",Les Nouvelles du Patchwork, France, 6/1997
"Broadway Haiku", Surface Design Journal, Winter, 1997
"American Art Quilts", Moscow Izvestia, April 4,1996
"Broadway Haiku", Quilts Japan, September, 1995
"Patterns of Vision", Art Quilt Magazine, Fall, 1995
"Art Quilt Calendar", Abbeville Press, 1995
"Brilliance In Color & Pattern", New York Times , April 24, 1994
"Shared Threads" by Jacqueline. Atkins, Penguin Publ., 1994
"The Quilts of Marilyn Henrion', Patchwork Tsushin, Japan, April, 1994
"Quilts:The Permanent Collection,Volume II",AQS Publ. 1994
"Les Poemes en Tissus de Marilyn Henrion", Les Nouvelles du Patchwork (France) April, 1994
"Tradition & Creativity In Quiltmaking", Patchwork Quilt Tsushin (Japan), April, 1994
"Quilts Composed As Poems In Cloth",New York Times, March 1, 1992

Curating

2012   "Be My Guest", multi-media group exhibition, gallery artists & invited guests, Noho Gallery, NYC, NY
2011   "Urban Landscapes", exhibition of works by eight fiber artists, Visions Art Museum, San Diego, CA
2004   "NOHO FIBER", Works by seven fiber artists, Noho Gallery, New York, NY
2003   "FIBRATIONS!": Works by Members of Art Quilt Network-NY, Noho Gallery, New York NY
1998   "Three Perspectives: Russian Fiber Artists", Tokyo International Forum, Tokyo, Japan
1996   "Five Perspectives: American Quilt Artists", Museum of Decorative & Applied Arts, Moscow, Russia
1995   "Ludmila Uspenskaya: Dreams & Fantasies", Museum of The American Quilters Society,Paducah, KY

Education

Cooper Union College for the Advancement of of Arts & Sciences, graduated 1952
Fordham University, BFA, 1972

www.ingramcontent.com/pod-product-compliance
Lightning Source LLC
Chambersburg PA
CBHW051104180526
45172CB00002B/765